My Little Book of Prayer

My Little Book of Prayer

S. M. Henriques

BRIGHTON BOOKS
Nashville, TN 37211
1-800-256-8584

ISBN 1-58334-034-3

Printed in the United States of America.

Layout by Swan Lake Communications, Jackson, Mississippi
Cover Design by Bart Dawson

For our
first grandchild,
who has yet to
be born.

Table of Contents

Introduction

Here is good news! God is waiting for you to talk to Him!

This little book will help you learn more about prayer. It will help you as you explore prayer and what it is all about.

But remember one very important thing: prayer is so much more than anybody could write about in a book.

But don't just take my word for it. Find out for yourself!

Talk to God. Tell Him what is on your mind. He can hear you!

Chapter 1

Can You Hear Me, God?

Dear God,
sometimes when
I pray, I'm not sure
that You hear me.
Help me to trust
You more.

You, LORD, give true peace
to those who depend on you,
because they trust you.
Isaiah 26:3 (NCV)

Dear God,
when I am lonely
and afraid,
help me to
trust You.
Help me believe
that You are near.

Even if I walk through a very dark
valley, I will not be afraid,
because you are with me.
Psalm 23:4 (NCV)

Dear God,
thank You
so much for
my family
and my home.

Do to others as you would
have them do to you.
Luke 6:31 (NIV)

Dear God,
please help me
to be kind to my
brothers and sisters.
Help me to love them
the way You love me!

Most importantly, love each
other deeply, because love will cause
many sins to be forgiven.
1 Peter 4:8 (NCV)

Dear God,
You are so good to me!
You have done such
wonderful things.
I am amazed when
I think of You!

I will praise the LORD at all times.
I will constantly speak his praises.
Psalm 34:1 (NLT)

Dear God,
thank You for
the beautiful
world You made!
Everything in it
is amazing!

I look at your heavens, which you made with your fingers. I see the moon and stars, which you created.
Psalm 8:3 (NCV)

Dear God,
help me to
understand that
sometimes Your
answer is much,
much better than
what I thought
it would be!

The LORD is wonderfully good to
those who wait for him and seek him.
Lamentations 3:25 (NLT)

Dear God,
please remind
me today
that I am
very precious
to You.

You are precious and
honored in my sight.
Isaiah 43:4 (NIV)

Dear God,

I love You
so much!

Love the Lord your God
with all your heart and with
all your soul and with all your
mind and with all your strength.
Mark 12:30 (NIV)

Chapter 2

What Is Prayer?

We can't see God, but we can still talk to Him.

Look to the LORD and his strength; seek his face always.
1 Chronicles 16:11 (NIV)

Talking to God is called "prayer."

Let us go right into the presence of God, with true hearts fully trusting him.
Hebrews 10:22 (NLT)

God really cares
about what is
going on in your life.
Tell Him about it.

"I know what I am planning for you," says the Lord. "I have good plans for you, not plans to hurt you. I will give you hope and a good future."
Jeremiah 29:11 (NCV)

Imagine that your prayer is like a fire. God sits in front of that fire and warms His hands.

The LORD is slow to anger
and rich in unfailing love.
Numbers 14:18 (NLT)

When you talk to God, imagine Him leaning down to put His ear close to your lips.

Now my eyes will be open
and my ears attentive to the
prayers offered in this place.
2 Chronicles 7:15 (NIV)

He wants to hear everything you say!

Then you will call upon me
and come and pray to me,
and I will listen to you.
Jeremiah 29:12 (NIV)

When you talk to God,
imagine a ladder
going up to God.
Then imagine
your prayers
going up
straight to God.

Hear the sound of my prayer,
when I cry out to you for help.
I raise my hands toward
your Most Holy Place.
Psalm 28:2 (NCV)

Everytime you put your hands together to pray, think of God opening His!

When you open your hand,
they are satisfied with good things.
Psalm 104:28 (NIV)

Imagine God walking right next to you, holding your hand in HIS!

Even if I walk through a very dark valley, I will not be afraid, because you are with me.
Psalm 23:4 (NCV)

ꟹ

Prayer is like knocking on the door of Heaven. God is always home.

Keep on asking, and you will be given what you ask for. Keep on looking, and you will find. Keep on knocking, and the door will be opened.
Matthew 7:7 (NLT)

ଓ

Prayer is a gift God gives to those who love Him.

If you remain in me and follow my teachings, you can ask anything you want, and it will be given to you.
John 15:7 (NCV)

Prayer helps us learn to trust God more.

As for me, I look to
the Lord for his help.
Micah 7:7 (NLT)

We can trust
Jesus with our
prayers, because
He is always
the same.

Jesus Christ is the same
yesterday and today and forever.
Hebrews 13:8 (NIV)

When we pray, we can feel God's peace surrounding us.

And God's peace, which is so great we cannot understand it, will keep your hearts and minds in Christ Jesus.
Philippians 4:6 (NCV)

Prayer is
a conversation
between
your heart
and
God's heart.

Hear my prayer, God;
listen to what I say.
Psalm 54:2 (NCV)

We like talking
to our best friends.
Prayer is talking to
the Best Friend
we could ever
have — God!

Devote yourselves to prayer with
an alert mind and a thankful heart.
Colossians 4:2 (NLT)

Stop
and think about it:
is there something
you should pray
about right now?

The LORD has heard my cry for help;
the LORD will answer my prayer.
Psalm 6:9 (NCV)

Chapter 3

Some Important Things To Remember About Prayer

God
is the one
Who answers
prayer.

. . . for you answer our prayers,
and to you all people will come.
Psalm 65:2 (NLT)

In fact,
God is the one
Who invented prayer
— just so we could
talk to Him!

Call to me and I will answer you
and tell you great and unsearchable
things you do not know.
Jeremiah 33:3 (NIV)

It is a good thing to pray with others, such as friends, family, and people at church.

Again, I tell you that if two of you
on earth agree about anything you
ask for, it will be done for
you by my Father in heaven.
Matthew 18:19 (NIV)

Jesus loves us!
That is why we can
trust Him enough
to talk to Him.
We can tell
Him anything!

Don't be troubled.
You trust God, now trust in me.
John 14:1 (NLT)

Prayer helps us remember that God is the one who helps us — so we do not need to be afraid.

So we can be sure when we say,
"I will not be afraid,
because the Lord is my helper.
People can't do anything to me."
Hebrews 13:6 (NCV)

God
really wants us
to pray when we
are in trouble.
He wants
to help us!

When they call on me, I will answer;
I will be with them in trouble.
I will rescue them and honor them.
Psalm 91:15 (NLT)

ɞ

God is near
to us when
we pray — no
matter where
we are!

The LORD is close to everyone
who prays to him, to all who
truly pray to him.
Psalm 145:18 (NCV)

In prayer we can ask God to forgive us for the wrong things we've done.

But if we confess our sins,
he will forgive our sins, because
we can trust God to do what is
right. He will cleanse us from all
the wrongs we have done.
1 John 1:9 (NCV)

The best prayers sometimes have no words at all.

Be still, and know that I am God;
I will be exalted among the nations,
I will be exalted in the earth.
Psalm 46:10 (NIV)

Turn off the TV and
close the door!
Too much noise can
keep us from hearing
what God wants
to say to us.

Be still in the presence of the LORD,
and wait patiently for him to act.
Psalm 37:7 (NLT)

We cannot hide anything from God. So go ahead and tell Him what is on your mind.

O LORD, you have examined my heart and know everything about me.
Psalm 139:1 (NLT)

Chapter 4

How Do I Pray?

Are you not sure what to say when you talk to God?

The Bible says that God will help you:

We do not know how
to pray as we should.
But the Spirit
himself speaks to
God for us, even begs
God for us with deep
feelings that words
cannot explain.

Romans 8:26 (NCV)

We don't have to be afraid when we pray.

In Christ we can come before God with freedom and without fear. We can do this through faith in Christ.
Ephesians 3:12 (NCV)

Here's a wonderful thought —

God wants to get closer to you!

Come near to God
and he will come near to you.
James 4:8 (NIV)

Don't worry.
Instead, tell God
what bothers you.

Don't worry about anything;
instead, pray about everything.
Tell God what you need, and thank
him for all he has done.
Philippians 4:6 (NLT)

ℬ

Jesus tells us to call God "Our Father."

So when you pray, you should pray like this: "Our Father in heaven, may your name always be kept holy."
Matthew 6:9 (NCV)

When you pray,
it's okay to sing
a song to God.

He would love
to hear your song!

Then you will sing psalms
and hymns and spiritual songs
among yourselves, making music
to the Lord in your hearts.
Ephesians 5:19 (NLT)

Remember to thank God for all the good things He has done for you.

Remember the miracles he has done,
his wonders, and his decisions.
1 Chronicles 16:12 (NIV)

Are you happy?

Tell God about it, and share your joy with Him.

My heart rejoices in the LORD!
Oh, how the LORD has blessed me!
1 Samuel 2:1 (NLT)

We've all done wrong. So we should ask God to forgive us.

Then if my people, who are
called by my name, are sorry for what
they have done, if they pray
and obey me and stop their evil ways,
I will hear them from heaven.
I will forgive their sin, and
I will heal their land.
2 Chronicles 7:14 (NCV)

When you pray, don't do it half-way. Instead, give it all you've got!

You will search for me.
And when you search for me
with all your heart, you will find me!
Jeremiah 29:13 (NCV)

In your prayers, thank God for the people you love.

I have not stopped giving thanks to God for you. I always remember you in my prayers.
Ephesians 1:16 (NCV)

You don't have
to use big words
when you pray.
Your prayer
doesn't have
to be long before
God will listen.
Just talk to Him.
Here's what
Jesus said:

"When you pray, don't be like those people who don't know God. They continue saying things that mean nothing, thinking that God will hear them because of their many words."

Matthew 6:7 (NCV)

Sometimes it helps to be alone when we pray.

When you pray, go away by yourself, shut the door behind you, and pray to your Father secretly.
Matthew 6:6 (NCV)

That's
what
Jesus
did!

Jesus often slipped away
to be alone so he could pray.
Luke 5:16 (NCV)

But we can pray
anywhere,
at any time,
and about
anything.

Pray in the Spirit on all occasions
with all kinds of prayers and requests.
Ephesians 6:18 (NIV)

Chapter 5

When Is A Good Time To Pray?

Pray when you need God to help you with a problem.

Depend on the LORD and his strength; always go to him for help.
1 Chronicles 16:11 (NCV)

Morning is a good time to pray.

LORD, every morning you hear my voice. Every morning, I tell you what I need, and I wait for your answer.
Psalm 5:3 (NCV)

Start each day with prayer.

Great is his faithfulness;
his mercies begin afresh each day.
Lamentations 3:23 (NLT)

At night,
talk to God about
the things that
happened during
the day.
Even at night,
He is listening!

I can lie down and go to sleep,
and I will wake up again, because the
LORD gives me strength.
Psalm 3:5 (NCV)

ജ

Sometimes Jesus prayed early in the morning.

Early the next morning, while it was still dark, Jesus woke and left the house. He went to a lonely place, where he prayed.
Mark 1:35 (NCV)

ଓ

Sometimes Jesus prayed all night.

Jesus went to a mountain to pray,
and he prayed to God all night.
Luke 6:12 (NLT)

Anytime of the day is a good time to pray!

Morning, noon, and night
I am troubled and upset,
but he will listen to me.
Psalm 55:17 (NCV)

It's always
a good idea
to pray just
before reading
your Bible.

Open my eyes that I may see
wonderful things in your law.
Psalm 119:18 (NIV)

When others do not understand you, or will not let you into their group, remember to pray before you do anything else!

The LORD does not look at the things man looks at. Man looks at the outward appearance, but the LORD looks at the heart.
1 Samuel 16:7 (NIV)

When you
feel all alone,
talk to God.

He loves you!

I am convinced that nothing
can ever separate us from his love.
Romans 8:38 (NLT)

Everyone feels
lonely sometimes.
Prayer helps us
to remember that
God is always with us,
and never forgets us!

God has said, "I will never leave you;
I will never forget you."
Hebrews 13:5 (NCV)

Are you afraid of the dark? Then read this verse from the Bible:

"You can lie
down without
fear and enjoy
pleasant dreams."

Proverbs 3:24 (NLT)

If you are being tempted to do wrong, remember that you can talk to God about it. He will not fuss at you!

Stay awake and pray for
strength against temptation.
The spirit wants to do what is right,
but the body is weak.
Matthew 26:41 (NCV)

We can pray anytime we need to.

God is always awake and listening.

Pray in the Spirit at all times with all kinds of prayers, asking for everything you need. To do this you must always be ready and never give up.
Ephesians 6:18 (NCV)

Are you having
a bad day?
Then read
what God
says
to you:

"But the people who
trust the LORD will
become strong again.
They will rise up
as an eagle in the sky;
they will run and
not need rest;
they will walk and
not become tired."

Isaiah 40:31 (NCV)

Never stop praying!

Keep on praying.
1 Thessalonians 5:17 (NLT)

Chapter 6

What Should I Pray About?

We can ask God for what we need.

Tell God what you need,
and thank him for all he has done.
Philippians 4:6 (NLT)

We should pray for others.

Always pray for all God's people.
Ephesians 6:18 (NCV)

Other people
have problems and
other things
that bother them.
Remember to pray
for them when
you talk to God.

You hear, O LORD, the desire
of the afflicted; you encourage them,
and you listen to their cry,
Psalm 10:17 (NIV)

Some people are very sick, and need our prayers.

Do you know someone who is very sick?

Therefore confess your sins to each other and pray for each other so that you may be healed. The prayer of a righteous man is powerful and effective.
James 5:16 (NIV)

Some people don't have a warm bed and good food to eat.

Be sure to pray for them, too!

Feed the hungry and help those in trouble. Then your light will shine out from the darkness, and the darkness around you will be as bright as day.
Isaiah 58:10 (NLT)

When we pray for others, sometimes God tells us what He wants us to do for them!

Therefore, as God's chosen people, holy and dearly loved, clothe yourselves with compassion, kindness, humility, gentleness and patience.
Colossians 3:12 (NIV)

Jesus prayed for the people who treated Him badly.

Jesus said,
"Father, forgive these people,
because they don't know
what they are doing."
Luke 23:34 (NLT)

We

should,

too!

But I say to you, love your enemies.
Pray for those who hurt you.
Matthew 5:44 (NCV)

We should pray for men and women who serve God in special ways.

Brothers, pray for us.
1 Thessalonians 5:25 (NIV)

Some of
these are
ministers,
missionaries,
teachers,
nurses,
and doctors.

We always thank God, the
Father of our Lord Jesus Christ,
when we pray for you.
Colossians 1:3 (NIV)

You can help your pastor by praying for him whenever he preaches. In fact, why not tell him that you are praying for him?

Also pray for me that when I speak, God will give me words so that I can tell the secret of the Good News without fear.
Ephesians 6:19 (NCV)

Missionaries serve God in other parts of the world by helping people there know about God.

I always want to preach the
Good News in places where people
have never heard of Christ.
Romans 15:20 (NCV)

Your teacher at school has a big job.

Write down a prayer for your teacher and leave it on her or his desk tomorrow.

Therefore encourage one another and build each other up.
1 Thessalonians 5:11 (NIV)

Doctors and nurses need our prayers, too.

They have a lot of sick people to take care of!

When a believing person prays,
great things happen.
James 5:16 (NCV)

Remember to pray for the president of our country, and others who lead us.

Pray for rulers and for all
who have authority so that we can
have quiet and peaceful lives full
of worship and respect for God.
1 Timothy 2:2 (NCV)

And, of course, we should pray for our parents, brothers and sisters!

Brothers and sisters, I beg
you to help me in my work
by praying to God for me.
Romans 15:30 (NCV)

Who are some people you need to remember to pray for?

I will surely not stop praying for you, because that would be sinning against the LORD.
1 Samuel 12:23 (NCV)

When we
talk to God,
we can ask Him
to show us the
right things to do.

Lord, tell me your ways.
Show me how to live.
Psalm 25:4 (NCV)

Always
be sure to say
"Thank You"
to God everytime
you pray. . .

Always give thanks to God
the Father for everything,
in the name of our Lord Jesus Christ.
Ephesians 5:20 (NCV)

. . . because we can never run out of things to thank God for!

Let your lives overflow with thanksgiving for all he has done.
Colossians 2:7 (NLT)

What are some things you can thank God for right now?

Now, our God, we give you thanks,
and praise your glorious name.
1 Chronicles 29:13 (NIV)

Don't put off
praying
to God.
Do it now!

Seek the Lord while he
may be found; call on him
while he is near.
Isaiah 55:6 (NIV)

What should you pray about?

Anything you want to!

But I keep right on
praying to you, LORD.
Psalm 69:13 (NLT)

Chapter 7

How Do We Know God Hears?

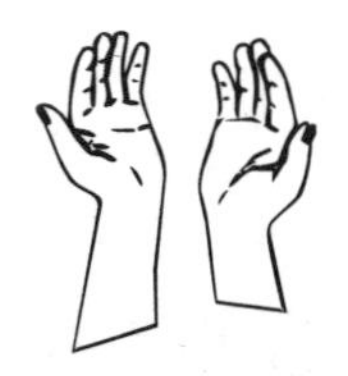

God hears us when we pray.

I have heard your prayer
and what you have asked me to do.
1 Kings 9:3 (NCV)

We can know that God hears us when we pray because nothing can pull us away from God's love.

I am convinced that nothing
can ever separate us from his love.
Romans 8:38 (NLT)

We know God answers prayer because the Bible says that God loves us always!

The Lord's love never ends;
his mercies never stop.
Lamentations 3:22 (NCV)

God can hear
our prayers — even
the ones we say in
our hearts so
no one else can hear.

Surely the Lord's power is
enough to save you. He can hear
you when you ask him for help.
Isaiah 59:1 (NCV)

If you are careful to obey everything He says, God will hear you when you pray.

The Lord . . . hears the prayers
of those who do right.
Proverbs 15:29 (NCV)

God says that if we obey Him, we can ask Him for what we need.

God gives us what we ask
for because we obey God's
commands and do what pleases him.
1 John 3:22 (NCV)

We know God hears us when we pray because He always keeps His promises.

Not one word has failed of all the wonderful promises he gave through his servant Moses.
1 Kings 8:56 (NLT)

"You know and fully believe that the LORD has done great things for you. You know that he has not failed to keep any of his promises."

Joshua 23:14 (NCV)

God is always listening, because He loves us very much!

The LORD sees the
good people and listens
to their prayers.
Psalm 34:15 (NCV)

God knows what we need even before we ask!

I will answer them before they even call to me. While they are still talking to me about their needs, I will go ahead and answer their prayers!
Isaiah 65:24 (NLT)

We don't know
all the different
ways that God
answers prayers.
But we know
He does!

For you answer our prayers,
and to you all people will come.
Psalm 65:2 (NLT)

CB

God
never falls asleep
on the job, nor is He
too busy to listen
to our prayers.

He will not let you
stumble and fall; the one who
watches over you will not sleep.
Psalm 121:3 (NLT)

The birds in the
sky remind us that
Jesus loves us
too much to
forget about us.
He hears our prayers,
and knows what
we need!

Look at the birds
of the air; they do
not sow or reap or
store away in barns,
and yet your heavenly
Father feeds them.
Are you not much
more valuable
than they?

Matthew 6:26 (NIV)

When you knock
on God's door,
He opens it
EVERY TIME . . .

. . . so don't be afraid to KNOCK!

For everyone who asks, receives.
Everyone who seeks, finds.
And the door is opened
to everyone who knocks.
Luke 11:10 (NLT)

So remember this: God is busy doing good things for you all the time!

And we know that God
causes everything to work
together for the good of those
who love God and are called
according to his purpose for them.
Romans 8:28 (NLT)

Chapter 8

What If I Don't Get What I Ask?

Sometimes
when we don't
get what we
ask, we might
think that God
doesn't hear us.

May the LORD answer
you in times of trouble.
Psalm 20:1 (NCV)

But God does hear us, and He always answers our prayers.

For as high as the heavens are
above the earth, so great is
his love for those who fear him.
Psalm 103:11 (NIV)

Sometimes God answers our prayers by saying "Yes!"

They blessed the king and then went home, joyful and glad in heart for all the good things the LORD had done.
1 Kings 8:66 (NIV)

Sometimes God answers our prayers by saying "No!"

The Lord is not slow
in doing what he promised —the way
some people understand slowness.
2 Peter 3:9 (NCV)

Sometimes God answers our prayers by saying "Wait!"

Keep yourselves in God's love as you wait for the Lord Jesus Christ with his mercy to give you life forever.
Jude 1:21 (NCV)

And sometimes God answers our prayers by saying "I've been waiting for you to ask Me!"

The ways of God are without fault. The Lord's words are pure. He is a shield to those who trust him.
Psalm 18:30 (NCV)

If we don't always get what we ask for, it may be because God has something much better in mind!

. . .the LORD knows what is in everyone's mind. He understands everything you think. If you go to him for help, you will get an answer.
1 Chronicles 28:9 (NCV)

Don't ask God for what you think is good; ask Him for what He thinks is good for you.

The LORD will work out
his plans for my life.
Psalm 138:8 (NLT)

If God gave us everything we asked Him for, sometimes we would get things that might hurt us . . .

How much more your heavenly Father will give good things to those who ask him!
Matthew 7:11 (NCV)

. . . so God has to say "No," because He loves us far too much to let us have some-thing that would not be good for us.

Therefore encourage each other with these words.
1 Thessalonians 4:18 (NIV)

Sometimes
what we think
is good
for us might
be bad for
someone else.

He blesses you with rain from above.
Genesis 49:25 (NCV)

We might pray
for a sunny day,
but God may know
that the earth
really needs rain!

God, you sent much rain; you
refreshed your tired land.
Psalm 68:9 (NCV)

So if God doesn't give you what you ask for, it's because He wants to give you something far, far better than anything you could ever imagine!

With God's power working in us, God can do much, much more than anything we can ask or imagine.
Ephesians 3:20 (NCV)

Chapter 9

A Few Words From God

Even when you do not know it, I am with you.

I will be your God throughout
your lifetime--until your hair is
white with age. I made you, and
I will care for you. I will carry you
along and save you.
Isaiah 46:4 (NLT)

If it looks as
though I have not
heard you, keep
praying and waiting.
I will answer!

Answer me when I pray to you,
my God who does what is right.
Make things easier for me when
I am in trouble. Have mercy on me
and hear my prayer.
Psalm 4:1 (NCV)

Look at the sky.
See how high it is?
That's how much
I love you!

For as high as the heavens are
above the earth, so great is his love
for those who fear him.
Psalm 103:11 (NIV)

My love
for you is
greater than
anything you
can imagine!

Christ's love is greater than
anyone can ever know, but I pray that
you will be able to know that love.
Ephesians 3:19 (NCV)

Learn to depend on Me for what you plan to do with your life.

Depend on the LORD in whatever you do, and your plans will succeed.
Proverbs 16:3 (NCV)

What I have said in the Bible can help keep you from doing wrong. Read it often.

I have hidden your word in my heart
that I might not sin against you.
Psalm 119:11 (NIV)

ꕥ

When you worship Me with all your heart, I will hear you and remind you of My love for you.

Children, come and listen to me.
I will teach you to worship the LORD.
Psalm 34:11 (NCV)

Every day,
take some time
to worship Me.
I want you to get
to know Me better.

Worship the LORD with gladness.
Come before him, singing with joy.
Psalm 100:2 (NLT)

I'll never get tired of hearing anything you have to tell Me.

But the love of the LORD remains forever with those who fear him.
Psalm 103:17 (NLT)

So talk to Me
anytime, anywhere
and about anything.

I'm listening!

I will provide for their needs before
they ask, and I will help them while
they are still asking for help.
Isaiah 65:24 (NCV)

About the Author

Dr. S. M. Henriques, known to his friends as "Rocky," lives and writes in Jackson, Mississippi. He is a graduate of New Orleans Baptist Theological Seminary, and has 20 years' experience as a pastor.

Rocky and his wife, Mary Ann, are the parents of two children, Jennifer and Jonathan.

He is the publisher of *The Timothy Report,* an electronic newsletter for pastors, church secretaries, church staff members, and Bible teachers.

For information about *The Timothy Report,* address your e-mail to SwanLC@aol.com.

Other books by S. M. Henriques
distributed by Walnut Grove Press:

God Can Handle It . . . Marriage
God Can Handle It For Kids
God Can Handle It Day By Day
Best Friends Last A Lifetime